The Chord Wheel
The Ultimate Tool for All Musicians
by Jim Fleser

T0047323

Quick Start Guide

More Applications

ISBN 978-0-634-02142-8

HAL•LEONARD®
CORPORATION

7777 W. BLUEMOUND RD. P.O. BOX 13819 MILWAUKEE, WI 53213

Patent pending for The Chord Wheel
www.chordwheel.com

Visit Hal Leonard Online at
www.halleonard.com

QUICK START GUIDE

The Chord Wheel is a revolutionary device that puts the most essential, practical applications of chord theory into your hands. *No music reading is necessary.* Simply rotate the transparent disk, and:

➤ Determine which chords belong to a given key and analyze any progression instantly.

➤ Transpose a chord progression to any key.

➤ Compose your own music.

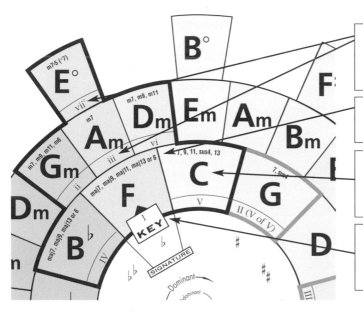

Roman numerals denote the harmonic progression. Upper-case numerals (I, IV, V) are major chords while lower-case (ii, iii, vi) are minor.

Sevenths and other extensions add color to a chord and make detailed analysis a breeze.

Chord names are also the major scale notes. The F major scale is thus F, G, A, B♭, C, D, E by counting I, ii, iii, IV, V, vi, vii for the notes.

Key is selected by aligning this box with the desired **tonic** (i.e., I chord). The number of sharps or flats corresponds to the key signature.

Analyzing Progressions

At the foundation of just about any composition is an underlying chord progression. The song's melody, and any improvisation played throughout, will be intimately tied to that underlying progression, so being able to analyze a progression in terms of key and Roman numerals is an essential skill for the improvising musician.

Step 1: Determining Key

Individually, most chords can belong to several keys; when combined into a progression, however, chords tend to work together to imply a single tonic or key center. This information can tell you what scale(s) to use for improvising over the entire progression, which greatly simplifies your job as a soloist. There are two ways to determine the "key" of a progression:

• Use your ears. Listen for the note or chord that sounds most "at rest"—often it's the first or last chord in the song or progression. This will be the "I chord" of the key. Be aware: This task can be next to impossible when dealing with complex progressions which may modulate through any number of keys.

• Use the Chord Wheel. By rotating the triangular outline printed on the transparent disk, you can easily determine a song's key: just turn the disk until all the chords (or as many as possible) are contained within the triangular pattern.

By using the Chord Wheel in conjunction with your ears, you'll be able to easily analyze even the most complex progressions.

Step 2: Assigning Roman Numerals

Once a key is determined, each chord can be assigned a Roman numeral (I, ii, V, etc.) based on its position and function within the key. There are several benefits to this knowledge:

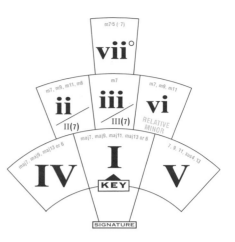

- By analyzing the theory behind your favorite composers or styles of music, you'll soon discover how each achieves the tension and release essential to effective composition. You'll realize, for example, how frequent modulations and liberal use of "ii-V-I" cadences typify many standard jazz progressions, while rock/blues-based tunes tend to rely on more stationary progressions, like "I-IV-V" changes.

- An accomplished soloist must be completely aware of a tune's framework to improvise effectively. Without this "roadmap," the improvisation will fail to follow along with a given song, and the result will be a solo that rambles on—or worse, sounds out of place.

- Communication between players frequently takes place at the theoretical level. Should a songwriting partner tell you that she'd like you to work on a song that "cycles forward along the circle of fifths utilizing a 'vi-ii-V7-I' cadence, but the bridge should modulate to somewhere harmonically distant such that it has an 'outside' sound," you'll be able to follow along effortlessly, whether you're recommending chord changes or laying down an eloquent solo.

Sample Progression, Part 1: The Verse

Verse:	Fmaj7	Dm	Gm7	C7
	Fmaj7	Dm9	Am	B♭

Above is a typical verse progression. Let's try analyzing it. Rotate the transparent disk on the Chord Wheel, searching for a key that contains as many of the above chords within the triangular outline as possible.

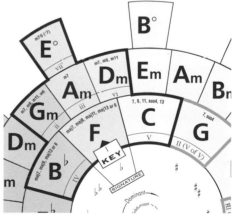

With a little trial and error, you'll eventually find that only one position contains all of the chords in the verse: the key of F (see right). We can therefore say that the verse of our sample progression is "in the key of F." Also, because the verse's chords all fit within the bold triangular outline without exceptions, it is completely within the key, or **diatonic**.

Key of F. When positioned here, each of the verse's chords are contained within the transparent disk's triangular outline.

Next, convert the verse to its **root progression**—that is, labeling the chords with the Roman numerals designated at the bottom of each cell. Take your time with this, then compare your results to the analysis below:

Key of F:	Imaj7	vi	ii7	V7
	Imaj7	vi9	iii	IV

Sample Progression, Part 2: The Chorus

Chorus:	Dm	G7	C	Cmaj7
	Am	D7	G	A7 Gmaj7

Now let's try the chorus. Again, after a little trial and error, you'll find that this section of the song is no longer in the key of F. In fact, there is no single key that contains all of the chords above. This indicates that the chorus either **modulates** to one or more other keys or contains at least one **accidental** (a chord outside the key). The strongest analysis indicates that the chorus modulates. The first half of the chorus is in the "key of C," and then we modulate to the "key of G" for the second half:

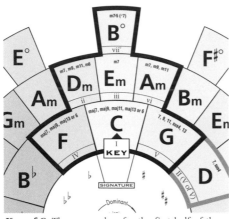

Key of C. The proper key for the first half of the chorus. All chords fall within the outline.

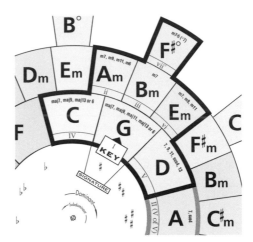

Key of G. The key for the second half of the chorus. Note that the A7 is not within the bold outline but in its own, fainter outline. Thus, it's not actually in the key (i.e., diatonic) but is still commonly used.

Harmonic (Root) Progression for the Chorus:

Key of C:	ii	V7	I	Imaj7
Key of G:	ii	V7	I	II7 Imaj7

Once you understand a progression like this through analysis, you have at your disposal a roadmap to great soloing. For instance, with the above progression, you could start by playing lines based on an F major scale during the verse, and then, when the chorus kicked in, employ licks based on the C major scale for the first four measures and the G major scale for the second half. Naturally, you'd want to add your favorite scale variations and pay attention to the **chord tones** (in other words, emphasize the notes that make up each chord, as opposed to just playing any and all the notes in a scale).

Analysis Tips

Modulations and Accidentals

While many popular songs remain entirely in one key, it's not unusual for a song to **modulate**—that is, to move to a different key or keys. This is especially true in jazz, which frequently modulates in and out of various keys throughout a given composition. In more traditionally structured music, you'll often find key modulations at points in the tune that musically "take the song somewhere else," such as a chorus or a bridge.

If, in the middle of a verse, there appears a chord that sounds like it came out of left field, it's probably out of key (often referred to as an **accidental**—though it's no accident!). It's important to remember that "out of key" does not imply incorrectness. In fact, many amazing songs are memorable because of their use of less predictable chords. What's important is that you know where these chords are coming from so they can become part of your ever-expanding musical vocabulary.

Common Chords

Perhaps you noticed that the first chord of the chorus, Dm, was also used in the verse (which we analyzed as being in a different key). This is not unusual: A given chord can belong to several keys. In fact, that's often part of why a verse and chorus work well together; they utilize some of the same chords. In this regard, *context* is essential in determining key. (By the way, these common chords are often referred to as **pivot chords** when used as transitions between keys.)

Unique Chords

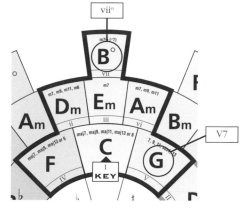

When analyzing a given progression, watch for chords that are unique to a given key. For example, anytime you see a **dominant seventh chord** (such as G7, D7, or A7), remember that it can only be diatonic to a single key, where it functions as a V7.

Likewise, the **vii° chord** (m7♭5) is also unique to each key. Thus anytime you see an F#° or F#m7♭5, for example, you know the only true corresponding key is the key of G.

Substitutions

One exception to the above rule: dominant seventh chords also happens to be a favorite chord type to use for substitutions. A **substitution** is a chord that "replaces" another chord in a given progression to add variety. A common substitution in jazz is the **tritone** or ♭**5** substitution. Rather than explain the theoretical details, think of the tritone as the chord on the exact opposite side of the Chord Wheel. It is most commonly applied to the V7 chord. So in the key of G, the tritone substitution for the V7 (D7) would be A♭7, as it is exactly opposite the D7. The tritone substitution for the ii7 (Am7) in this key would be an E♭m7. As with any substitution, a dominant seventh chord is often used. As you accumulate a knowledge of substitutions, you'll see how the Chord Wheel outlines them visually, making them easy to utilize.

Transposition

Let's face it, transposing progressions from one key to another is a necessary skill for all musicians. There are numerous instances in which transposition comes in handy:

- When accompanying a vocalist who needs a song played in a lower (or higher) range.
- When arranging for instruments in non-concert tuning.
- When modulating up a step midway through a tune to add excitement.
- When playing with a capo on your guitar, and then communicating that progression to other musicians.

The list could go on and on.

Once you've analyzed a progression, the Chord Wheel makes transposing it to a different key a snap. Simply rotate the transparent disk to the new key and, using the Roman numerals at the bottom of each chord's box, convert the progression into the chords of the new key. (If you like, you can write directly on the transparent disk; it was designed for use with a dry erase marker.) Chord types such as "m7" and "maj9" remain the same.

Try transposing our previous sample progression such that the verse starts in the "key of G," and check your results below. NOTE: When transposing a modulation, just recognize how many keys away the new key is form the original. In this example, the modulations each take the wheel one step clockwise.

	Original Key			
Verse:	Fmaj7	Dm	Gm7	C7
	Fmaj7	Dm9	Am	B♭
Chorus:	Dm	G7	C	Cmaj7
	Am	D7	G	A7 Gmaj7

	Harmonic Analysis			
Key of F:	Imaj7	vi	ii7	V7
	Imaj7	vi9	iii	IV
Key of C:	ii	V7	I	Imaj7
Key of G:	ii	V7	I	II7 Imaj7

	Transposed Key			
Key of G:	Gmaj7	Em	Am7	D7
	Gmaj7	Em9	Bm	C
Key of D:	Em	A7	D	Dmaj7
Key of A:	Bm	E7	A	B7 Amaj7

Composition

The Chord Wheel is especially valuable when composing your own progressions. Chords located completely within a single key's triangular pattern are said to be "diatonic" and will sound very much like they belong together. Moving outside the key's chord family will result in adding more tension to a song (often very desirable). By gaining better control of the "tension and release" inherent in the movement of chords and the art of modulation, you'll have the tools necessary for inventive composition.

As a musician, you may come up with a small bit of a composition (such as a "hook" or "riff") and, liking the sound of it, wish to expand it into a complete song. Instead of randomly playing additional chords, hoping to stumble across something that catches your ear, you can now focus in on the sounds implied by the notes/chords already established by the riff.

As an example, let's say that you've come up with a bit that revolves around three chords: Am, C, and G. Rotate the transparent disk until these three chords are contained within the outline. You'll find that you could theoretically be playing in three different keys depending on how you interpret your progression.

Original Chords Used: Am, C, and G.

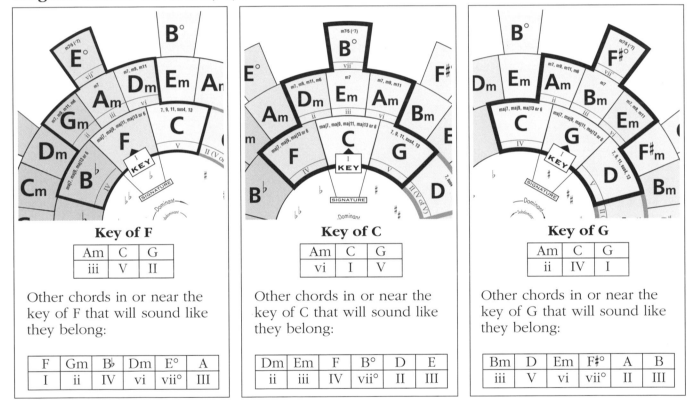

Key of F

Am	C	G
iii	V	II

Other chords in or near the key of F that will sound like they belong:

F	Gm	B♭	Dm	E°	A
I	ii	IV	vi	vii°	III

Key of C

Am	C	G
vi	I	V

Other chords in or near the key of C that will sound like they belong:

Dm	Em	F	B°	D	E
ii	iii	IV	vii°	II	III

Key of G

Am	C	G
ii	IV	I

Other chords in or near the key of G that will sound like they belong:

Bm	D	Em	F#°	A	B
iii	V	vi	vii°	II	III

The key (or keys) in which you decide to interpret the progression is up to you. One way to determine very quickly in which key you personally are hearing the chords is by adding more notes to the existing chords. Try playing the C in your new progression as a major seventh (Cmaj7) and then as a dominant seventh (C7). If the Cmaj7 sounds like it fits, then the key of C or the key of G is where to start. If the C7 sounds closer to what you're hearing, then continue your composition in the key of F.

Visit the Chord Wheel website at www.chordwheel.com *for greater detail regarding using this product as a composition aide. There you will find a comprehensive tutorial and more detailed discussions on other topics as well.*

Typical Chords and Progressions

When writing or playing a song in the key of C, you can see that we can play the chords C, F, and G as a progression and expect them to sound solidly "in key." In fact, the results sound very good; as if the chords belonged together. If you analyze C, F, and G with your Chord Wheel, you will find that they translate as the I chord, the IV chord, and the V chord in the key. Have you ever heard somebody mention a "one-four-five progression"? What they were really saying was "I-IV-V." These are probably the three most common chords in all of music. For one thing, they're the basis of the renowned "twelve-bar blues," which in turn is the foundation of much rock and jazz.

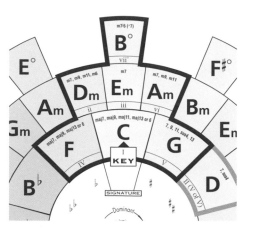

Primary Chords

I, **IV**, and **V** could be said to be the **primary chords** in any major key. The first chord, the I chord, is the defining chord of the key and is also called the **tonic**. It is consistently the most utilized chord, regardless of key, and most other chords in a key's "family" will tend to make the listener's ears ache to hear resolution to it. Use this expectation to pull listeners along as well as provide them with the comfortable resolution they desire.

After the I chord, the most characteristic sound of a given key is the V chord, called the **dominant**. At the very center of the Chord Wheel, you'll discover a clockwise arrow indicating the direction of the dominant. Among the strongest of listener tendencies recognized by music theorists is the "movement to dominant." Simply stated, our ears seem to possess an inherent expectation that musical tones want to progress from a root, or tonic, to the note a "fifth" higher, which would be the root of the V chord. The V chord, in turn, makes the listener expect to hear resolution back to the I chord, particularly when it's voiced as a dominant seventh (V7), a unique chord in the key.

The IV chord, called the **subdominant**, also works to draw the listener away from, and back to, the tonic. It's a more relaxed sound but very effective. The counterclockwise arrow at the center of the Chord Wheel indicates the direction of the subdominant. One characteristic of the IV chord is that, like the tonic (I chord), it can be a major seventh (maj7) chord. Thus if you come across a major seventh chord in a progression, it can be functioning as the tonic (the I chord) or the subdominant (the IV chord), depending on context or interpretation.

Secondary Chords

Notice that the innermost circle of the Chord Wheel consists of a given key's major chords (I, IV, and V), while the middle circle contains the key's minor chords (ii, iii, and vi) and the outer circle contains the key's one diminished (vii°) chord.

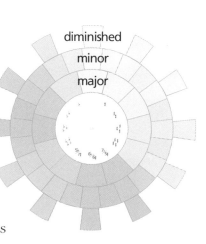

diminished
minor
major

Of course, keys have been settled upon because *all* the chords formed by their component notes sound good together—including the chords **ii**, **iii**, **vi**, and **vii°**. These could be considered the **secondary chords** of a major key; they're not as crucial in establishing the key center, but they're valuable nonetheless—they represent "somewhere else to go" in a major key. As you can see, most of them are minor. This means they're less consonant but also more colorful.

A particularly common element of many jazz progressions is the "ii-V-I cadence." Though it sounds complex, a ii-V-I in the key of C is simply Dm, G, and C. Likewise, a favorite progression of old time rock 'n' roll was I-vi-IV-V, which translates as C-Am-F-G in the key of C.

The II & III Chords

Most pop tunes stay within a single key—practically the entire Bob Dylan catalog, for example. Others modulate. Some add just the "II" or "III" chords. Though the II and III chords aren't actually diatonic to a major key, study the chord progressions of The Beatles, Rolling Stones, Elvis Costello, etc., and you'll discover that, without taking these two chords into consideration, their progressions would be utterly confusing.

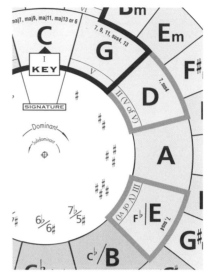

The II and III chords sound great for variety. And believe it or not, there's actually a theoretical reason for their inclusion; they're popular **secondary dominants**. What that means is, they can "act" like dominant V chords to other chords within the key. The II chord (D in the key of C) can act like the "V" of the V chord (G), while the III chord (E) can act like the "V" of vi (Am). You don't need to know this to use them, however. Just use your ears and experiment.

The Circle of Fifths

If we start with C, and continue to take dominant after dominant (C to G to D to A, etc.), you'll notice that after just twelve notes, we return back to our starting point. This cyclical nature is called the **circle of fifths** (or alternately, the circle of fourths) and is one of the most fundamental principles in all of music theory. The circle of fifths is at the foundation of the Chord Wheel, making up its innermost ring (where all of the major chords are found). A few aspects are worth noting:

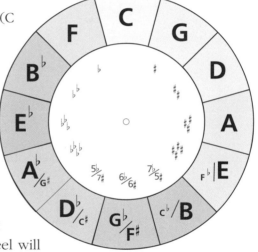

- Modulations often move one "key" clockwise (or counter-clockwise) on the circle of 5ths. This is due to the strong pull of tonic to dominant, and vice versa. Such neighboring keys also have many chords in common, as the Chord Wheel will confirm.

- Though the subdominant is generally looked at as the IV chord of a given key, the term "subdominant" actually implies that the "movement to dominant" is such a strong tendency that our ears might instead hear the IV as being a chord of resolution. For example, consider the progression C-F. While it's I-IV in the key of C, in the key of F, it's V-I. So the F chord can sound like a IV or a I, depending on interpretation. Both ways of seeing it are valid. Here's the point: Instead of thinking of moving counterclockwise along the circle of fifths as going from I to IV, consider that it can also be interpreted as going from V to I.

Key Signatures and Enharmonics

You should be familiar with key signatures. Simply put, a **key signature** is a representation of the number of notes in a given key (and thus the notes of its related scale) that are sharped or flatted. Turn the clear plastic disk on your Chord Wheel so that the "KEY-I Chord" arrow is aligned with D. You'll see the key signature of D has two sharps. Likewise, two of the chords in the key of D have sharps: the iii chord (F♯m) and the vii chord (C♯m).

Now examine the "key of G♭" on the Chord Wheel. Notice that it also can be expressed as the "key of F♯." These two notes, G♭ and F♯, are identical on any musical instrument. They're two names for the exact same tone. This property is called being **enharmonic** (a fancy word that means "sounds exactly the same"). Just as the note F♯ could also be called G♭, the two keys are identical.

MORE APPLICATIONS

Scales

As you may or may not know, a **scale** is a set of notes (usually seven) arranged in series, from one note to the same note an octave higher. Think, "Do, re, mi, fa, so, la, ti, do."

C	D	E	F	G	A	B	C*
do	re	mi	fa	so	la	ti	do

Scales are the raw material of melodic improvisation. With the Chord Wheel, you have access to any major scale right at your fingertips; just find the corresponding major key, take the letter name of each chord, and arrange the notes in numerical order.

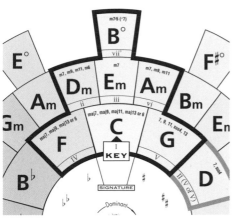

For example, grab your Chord Wheel and align the movable transparent disk to the "key of C." Now, using just the Roman numerals for the time being (paying no attention to whether they are upper or lower-case, and ignoring any lower-case "m's"), arrange the notes of C major in order:

Notes of the C major scale:

Key	I	ii	iii	IV	V	iv	vii
C	C	D	E	F	G	A	B

Voila! Your first scale!

Now try doing the same after aligning the Chord Wheel's transparent disk to the "key of D." Just go "I, ii, iii, IV, V, vi, vii," and you'll have the scale of D major.

Notes of the D major scale:

Key	I	ii	iii	IV	V	iv	vii
D	D	E	F♯	G	A	B	C♯

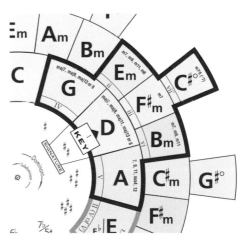

If you're having trouble placing the notes in proper order, refer to the Roman numeral equivalency chart below. And, by the way, if this seems like a lot of work to determine the notes in a scale, don't worry. It's not a question you'll need to be asking yourself frequently to exercise the practical benefits of chord theory; you'll eventually memorize many of these basics.

Number	1	2	3	4	5	6	7
Roman numeral (upper case)	I	II	III	IV	V	VI	VII
Roman numeral (lower case)	i	ii	iii	iv	v	vi	vii

---

* The beginning note of a scale is much lower in tone than the finishing note, but due to the way our ears hear music they sound almost identical. This pattern repeats over and over, both up and down. (This cyclical behavior is common in music theory and is a principal reason the Chord Wheel is constructed the way it is.)

Chords

We know how to find the chords in a key, and the notes in a scale, but how do you know what notes make up a chord? It's really pretty simple. First off, all chords are built in **thirds**. In scale terms, that translates into **every other note** of a scale.

Triads

The most basic chord type is called a **triad**; it contains three notes. A triad is put together by taking any note in a scale as a starting point (called the **root** of the chord) and then adding two more notes—the **3rd** and the **5th**—in an "every other note" manner. So, if we were starting from the first note in the C major scale (C, which we'll number as "1"), we would skip a note and add the next scale note instead: the note numbered "3," which is E. If we once again skip a note ("4") and add the "5" note, G, we have all three notes of our triad: C, E, G. This is C major, the I chord in the key.

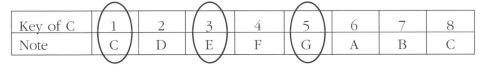

Try the same thing starting from the second note of the scale, D. Using our "every other note" pattern, we know that our triad will contain the 2nd, 4th and 6th notes of the major scale: D, F, A. This turns out to be a D minor chord, the ii chord in the key:

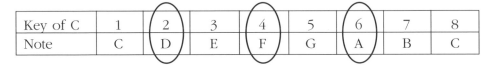

You can use this method to spell any chord in the key of C major, or any other key for that matter. Remember, start at any Roman numeral and pick every other numeral counting up—keeping in mind that when you get to what would be "eight," you simply start over again at "one." Another great way to do this is always knowing that the "every other note" pattern is going to provide notes with "every other" letter. When you go past G, just start over again at A. The only thing left is to figure out if any notes happen to be sharps (♯'s) or flats (♭'s), and the Chord Wheel can tell you that!

Major vs. Minor (vs. Diminished)

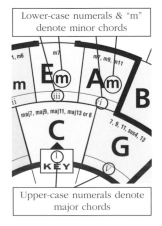

The Chord Wheel tells us that a C chord is major and a Dm chord is minor, but it doesn't tell us why. You may well ask, "What's the difference between a major and a minor chord?"

Start out with the tonic chord of the key of C, which is C major. As we covered already, the actual notes are C, E, and G. Now, using the Chord Wheel, let's compare it to Cm, which happens to be the ii chord in the key of B♭ (aligning the transparent disk to the of B♭ will confirm this). Start at ii (or the 2nd) in the key of B♭ and take every other note (the 4th and 6th), and you can see the C minor chord is made up of the notes C, E♭, and G.

So if C major is made up of the notes C, E, and G, while C minor is made up of C, E♭, and G, what is the difference? Even though each chord is built on a different scale degree within its respective key, both chords are built in thirds, and both are said to consist of a root, 3rd, and 5th. In the minor chord, the 3rd is an E♭, while in the major, it's an E. Thus, the 3rd of the minor chord is **flatted**. (The E and E♭ are a different note by one degree on any musical instrument, whether it be one piano key or one fret of a guitar. This difference is the smallest measurement used in western music and is referred to as a **half step**.)

What about the diminished (vii°) chord? The diminished chord goes "one step further" than the minor chord: It flats the 5th of the chord as well. So a C diminished triad would consist of the notes C, E♭, and G♭. (You can check this spelling by turning the Chord Wheel to the key of D♭, where C° functions as the vii° chord.) The diminished chord has a harsh, dissonant quality, due to the ♭5, and that makes it one of the "lesser-used" chord types in popular music.

type	formula	note names	chord name
major	1-3-5	C-E-G	C
minor	1-♭3-5	C-E♭-G	Cm
diminished	1-♭3-♭5	C-E♭-G♭	C°

NOTE: Many music students find the above "formula method" confusing, because it defines a minor chord (with its flatted 3rd) by comparing it to a major chord/scale. The Chord Wheel allows for you to enjoy the benefits of chord theory without intimate knowledge of this type. If the above formulas seem confusing, simply refer to any of the numerous texts on how to play chords on your given instrument. When getting started, it's more important to know *when* a C chord is played (as opposed to a Cm or C°), and which to solo with, than it is to grasp the differences in their construction.

Seventh Chords

If a triad contains three notes, what happens if we add another note to a chord? If we continue to utilize our "every other note" pattern from the tonic, we get the 1st, 3rd, 5th, and 7th notes of the scale. Thus we get a **seventh chord**. Make sense?

There are three basic types of seventh chords: **major seventh** (maj7), **dominant seventh** (7), and **minor seventh** (m7). The first two are built from adding the 7th to a major triad, and the last is built from a minor triad. The difference between the major seventh and dominant seventh is a half step, but it's how they sound and are used that's important.

Of course, the Chord Wheel tells us what type of seventh goes with each chord in a key—so if we were playing the chords C, F, and G (I, IV, V in the key of C) and wanted to play the chords as sevenths to add more flavor, the Chord Wheel would prompt us with the appropriate type (Cmaj7, Fmaj7, and G7). If we need help spelling seventh chords, the notes for each are contained within the triangular outline, just as they were for triads.

What about the minor seven flat-five (m7♭5), a.k.a half-diminished chord (°7)? This, once again, is a lesser-used chord in popular music. It can be seen as an alteration of the minor seventh, but diatonically functions as an extension of the diminished (vii°) triad.

type	formula	note names	chord name
major seventh	1-3-5-7	C-E-G-B	Cmaj7 (or C△7)
dominant seventh	1-3-5-♭7	C-E-G-B♭	C7
minor seventh	1-♭3-5-♭7	C-E♭-G-B♭	Cm7
minor seven flat-five	1-♭3-♭5-♭7	C-E♭-G♭-B♭	Cm7♭5 (or C°7)

Ninths, Elevenths, and Thirteenths

After absorbing the previous chord theory information, it should be easy to determine what a ninth chord is. Adding one more note in our "every other note in the scale" pattern (that is, 1st, 3rd, 5th, 7th), the next note would be the "9th." The same holds true for eleventh and thirteenth chords. Note that due to our "every other" pattern, all the chord extensions are odd numbers. When dealing with chords extended beyond the 7th, you'll often find that the chords are played without all the notes being represented. Why? Because six or seven notes can make a single chord sound cluttered and even unplayable. For example, a 9th chord will often be played without the root, as it can be assumed that note will be taken care of in the bass register.

The Relative Minor (and Other Modes)

So far we've only covered major scales and keys. While they are by far the most widely used, there are as many scales as you can imagine—one day, you may even develop your own! The other three most common scales are natural minor, melodic minor, and harmonic minor. Theoretically, each one could have its own Chord Wheel. However, the "vi chord" is unique in that it can be considered the primary chord (the tonic) of the natural minor scale/key, also called the **relative minor**.

Let's say you find a progression like the following:

Verse:	Am	C	Dm	E
	Am	G	F	E

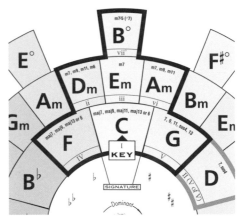

While we could say that this progression fits in the key of C—all of its chords fit within that framework—it certainly doesn't spend much time on I or V. Instead, each phrase begins on the "vi" chord (Am), and the "III" chord (E) is featured prominently—not just as a color chord. What's more, the "I" chord, C, really doesn't sound much like the tonic of the progression.

This is a great example of a progression in the relative minor—in this case, A minor. The key of A minor uses the same chords as C major—and therefore the same triangular outline on the Chord Wheel (hence the word, *relative*)—but it emphasizes different chords within that family. In the relative minor, the vi chord actually feels like the tonic, or center, of the key. In this regard, the ii and the iii or III chords will function as the subdominant and dominant. Try developing compositions based around the somber tones of the vi, ii, and iii chords, and you'll soon get a feel for this; you'll be working in the relative minor.

Incidentally, the same principle can apply to any chord in a major key, and that's where the concepts of **modes** begins. If a chord other than the major or relative minor feels like the tonic, then we consider the progression to be "in a mode." Typically, unless altered chords are used, the Chord Wheel can still apply, as each mode makes use of the exact same family of chords, just emphasized differently.

Tonic:	I	ii	iii	IV	V	vi	vii°
Mode:	Ionian	Dorian	Phrygian	Lydian	Mixolydian	Aeolian	Locrian
	(major)					(minor)	

While this text has been provided to get you up and running, music is a subject of unlimited depth. Please visit the website at www.chordwheel.com *for greater detail concerning the essential applications of chord theory and for further discussions regarding the use of this invaluable tool.*